Mathematics and Computing/Technology
An Inter-faculty Second Level Course

MT262 Putting Computer Systems to Work

Block II

Structures

Unit 1

Records and Arrays

Prepared for the Course Team by Alan Best

This text forms part of the Open University second-level course MT262 *Putting Computer Systems to Work*, which among other things teaches the use of Borland C++Builder 5 Standard to tackle small programming projects. (Borland C++Builder 5 Standard is copyright © 2000 Borland International (UK) Limited.)

The course software comprises the Borland C++Builder 5 Standard CD-ROM and the MT262 Templates and Libraries CD-ROM, both of which are supplied as part of the course.

This publication forms part of an Open University course. Details of this and other Open University courses can be obtained from the Student Registration and Enquiry Service, The Open University, PO Box 197, Milton Keynes, MK7 6BJ, United Kingdom: tel. +44 (0)870 333 4340, e-mail general-enquiries@open.ac.uk

Alternatively, you may visit the Open University website at http://www.open.ac.uk where you can learn more about the wide range of courses and packs offered at all levels by The Open University.

To purchase a selection of Open University course materials, visit the webshop at www.ouw.co.uk, or contact Open University Worldwide, Michael Young Building, Walton Hall, Milton Keynes, MK7 6AA, United Kingdom, for a brochure: tel. +44 (0)1908 858785, fax +44 (0)1908 858787, e-mail ouwenq@open.ac.uk

The Open University, Walton Hall, Milton Keynes, MK7 6AA.

First published 1999. Second edition 2002.

Copyright © 2002 The Open University

All rights reserved; no part of this publication may be reproduced, stored in a retrieval system, transmitted or utilised in any form or by any means, electronic, mechanical, photocopying, recording or otherwise, without written permission from the publisher or a licence from the Copyright Licensing Agency Ltd. Details of such licences (for reprographic reproduction) may be obtained from the Copyright Licensing Agency Ltd, 90 Tottenham Court Road, London W1T 4LP.

Open University course materials may also be made available in electronic formats for use by students of the University. All rights, including copyright and related rights and database rights, in electronic course materials and their contents are owned by or licensed to The Open University, or otherwise used by The Open University as permitted by applicable law.

In using electronic course materials and their contents you agree that your use will be solely for the purposes of following an Open University course of study or otherwise as licensed by The Open University or its assigns.

Except as permitted above you undertake not to copy, store in any medium (including electronic storage or use in a website), distribute, transmit or re-transmit, broadcast, modify or show in public such electronic materials in whole or in part without the prior written consent of The Open University or in accordance with the Copyright, Designs and Patents Act 1988.

Edited, designed and typeset by The Open University, using the Open University TeX System.

Printed in the United Kingdom by Martins the Printers, Berwick-upon-Tweed

ISBN 0 7492 4056 3

2.2

Contents

Study guide

A recommended study pattern, based on an average overall study time, is as follows.

Material	Study time
Introduction, Section 1 (text)	2 hours
Section 2 (text)	3 hours
Section 3 (computer)	3 hours
Section 4 (computer)	3 hours

You will need access to your computer whilst studying Sections 3 and 4.

The template files and course team solution files associated with the computing activities are to be found in the `Block II` subfolder of MT262. This subfolder is part of the MT262 Templates and Libraries software that you installed in *Unit 1*, Block I. The first computer activity, in Section 3, will guide you in making `Block II` the active folder.

Introduction

In Block I you encountered a handful of data types with which computer programs have to work, and looked at the various operations associated with each. The types integer, real, character and boolean are known as **basic** types. By and large, you can use these types without concern about how the computer stores such values and how it carries out operations involving them. The string type was seen to be more complex than the above four types, but it is still regarded as a basic data type. One convenient way of visualising a string value is as a sequence of characters (in a prescribed order), and to manipulate string values requires access to the individual characters making up the string. Computer languages implement strings in numerous different ways. Indeed, in C++ there are no fewer than three recognised ways of implementing a string, one of which is the *AnsiString* that you have been using. In *Unit 3*, you will discover that there is much more to *AnsiString* than might be anticipated. Each *AnsiString* variable is an example of an **object** and comprises much more than the characters making up its value.

Unfortunately, the data needed to model real-life situations is rarely of just *one* of the basic types already mentioned. Consider, for example, the task of maintaining customer accounts at a bank. What type of data would be used to represent a bank account?

In fact, a bank account comprises a number of individual items of information, one possible listing being the following.

> name, address, telephone number, account number, PIN
> age
> credit limit, balance

No doubt your bank manager holds different bits of information in connection with your account.

Each of these attributes can be represented by one of the basic data types. The first five listed could be declared to be of type string, the sixth of type integer and the final two each of type real. Although the bank account, as visualised here, consists of eight individual items of data, the items 'belong together'. Corresponding to one bank account, there will be eight related items of data.

A PIN number might need to be changed, but it will not be added to another such number; hence string is an appropriate type.

What is needed for this situation is a new data type called *AccountType*, say, which encompasses the eight interrelated items that make up the whole. One of the important features of most high-level programming languages is that they allow the programmer to create such **structured** types, that is, complex types of data which are built up from existing types. An initialised variable of type *AccountType* will hold, somehow, eight constituent values for a particular account. But the bank is not concerned with just one instance of an account; there will presumably be one variable of type *AccountType* for each customer.

The creation of the *AccountType* data type will certainly help with the problem of maintaining bank accounts. It will be necessary to have operations on this type of data, so that the individual values can be initialised, read and updated as necessary.

This block is concerned with such structured data types. As you progress through the block, you will appreciate that these creations need not consist of data in isolation. As for the basic data types, the operations on structured data types need to be specified. This all leads to the concept of an **object**, which is a collection of data items together with methods (operations) to manipulate those data items.

This first unit begins to build new structured data types by introducing two new concepts. In Section 1, the ideas illustrated by the bank account example are formalised by introducing **records**. Section 2 moves on to tackle the need to represent collections of data items of the *same* sort. For this purpose, **arrays** are used. Putting the two notions together as an array of records, to form what is called a **table**, provides a convenient way of storing large quantities of data. The table concept is the basis of most databases, and hence of considerable importance. In terms of the customer accounts at a bank, the collection of all such accounts, each of which is a record of type *AccountType*, is an example of a table (or an array of records).

The problem of efficient storage and retrieval of data has been a source of programming activity for many years. Numerous algorithms have been created for searching and sorting databases. The course will not get involved in a detailed study of such matters but, as illustrative examples, one searching algorithm and one sorting algorithm will be discussed in the context of data stored in a table. These algorithms require the third type of loop — the unconditioned **for** loop. Section 3 introduces this loop and looks at some typical situations in which its use is preferred to a conditioned loop. The **for** loop will then be applied in the algorithms for searching and sorting tables that form the subject matter of Section 4.

1 Records

The example of a bank account mentioned in the Introduction serves to illustrate the need to draw together data items of different types, into groups forming single, more complex entities. The basic structure for this purpose is that of a **record**. Records are introduced here by using an example that is not quite so complicated as the bank account.

1.1 Designing records

Suppose that the secretary of a tennis club keeps details of club membership on a card index system. A typical card entry is as illustrated in the following figure.

Peter Wilson	123 Main Street, Newtown
	AB1 2CD
M	
32	01234 567890

The secretary has used some shorthand here and knows to interpret the six given items of information (by virtue of their positions on the card) as being the name, address, postcode, gender (M for male and F for female), age and telephone number of this particular member.

The telephone number would be a string, not an integer.

All the information relates to one entity (here a member of the club) but its components are of differing types; four are of string type, one (age) is an integer and one (gender) a single character.

Suppose that it is decided to create a template index card so that during the secretary's absence someone else could fill out a new card. The template would tell users which six bits of information are needed, and where to enter them on the card. It might look something like the following.

Name......	Address...............
	PostCode..............
Gender....	
Age.......	TeleNo................

The programming equivalent of this template card is called a **record type definition**.

You will see an example of such a definition shortly.

The template and the record type definition can be regarded as having six distinct parts, each of which is called a **field**. Each field is distinguished by its own identifier: *Name*, *Address*, *PostCode*, *Gender*, *Age* or *TeleNo*. The field identifiers, and the types of data associated with them, determine the **record structure**. Corresponding to an actual card (containing information about a particular member), there is a **record variable** of the appropriate record type.

To emphasise the role of the fields, the record variable containing information on Peter Wilson can be illustrated as follows.

PWRecord

Name	Peter Wilson
Address	123 Main Street, Newtown
PostCode	AB1 2CD
Gender	M
Age	32
TeleNo	01234 567890

This record variable has been given an identifier, namely *PWRecord*. It is one instance of the tennis club membership record type. There will be many more instances, presumably one for each member, and each will require a unique identifier.

The record variable referenced by the single identifier *PWRecord* is essentially a collection of six variables.

To work with records (or other programmer-defined data types) there will always be two stages: defining the data type and declaring each variable of that type. The idea of type definitions (for records and other data types) needs to be incorporated into the design stage for problems. The course team has chosen to separate type definitions from the main data table.

Suppose that the tennis club membership record type is to be called *MemberType*. The index card template translates into a (record) type definition as follows. It is described below.

Structure definition	*MemberType*	
Type	Field identifier	Description
String	*Name*	First name and surname
String	*Address*	Address to town level
String	*PostCode*	Postcode in standard format
Character	*Gender*	Gender 'M' or 'F'
Integer	*Age*	Age at last birthday
String	*TeleNo*	Telephone number in 01234 567890 format

What has been done here has been known, historically, as making a **type definition**, but C++ uses the term **structure definition** and this course will do so too, at the design stage as well as the coding stage. The first row of the table clarifies that this is a structure definition of the type *MemberType*. Then a listing of the fields is given, each accompanied by its type and a brief description of its role. The **type name** *MemberType* is just another identifier; any such identifier should conform to the same rules as used for an identifier of a variable of basic type. The course team will always use type name identifiers that end in *Type* to distinguish them from basic variable identifiers, and you are strongly recommended to do the same, especially when submitting work for assessment.

The listing of the fields resembles a data table.

Variables of this record type can then be recorded in a data table in the usual way.

Type	Identifier	Description
MemberType	*PWRecord*	A record variable of the defined type
MemberType	*NextRecord*	Another record variable of the defined type

Try the following exercises, which are designed to make you think about organisation of data. Do not worry if you have no idea how you might use the structures you are asked to create; that comes next.

Exercise 1.1 _____

In a program concerned with employees of a certain company, it is decided to use a record structure to hold information about employees. Each record will hold the name, department, number of years of completed service, marital status and current annual salary of an employee. Make a structure definition of a type *EmployeeType* for such a record in the form of the table above. You will need to decide appropriate types for the five fields.

Exercise 1.2 _____

In a certain software package the monitor screen is regarded as forming 80 columns and 25 rows for the purpose of displaying characters. The cursor may be in any one of $80 \times 25 = 2000$ positions on the screen. The top left corner of the screen is the position with column 1 and row 1, and the bottom right corner of the screen is the position with column 80 and row 25. Design a record structure that will hold the current cursor position on the screen.

Exercise 1.3 _____

An entry to the National Lottery involves selection of six distinct integers in the range from 1 to 49 inclusive, together with an indication of how many draws the entry is to cover (from 1 to 8 inclusive), and whether the entry is for the Wednesday draw alone, the Saturday draw alone, or both draws. The entry starts from the next draw after the current date. Design a record structure to contain the information needed for such a lottery entry.

[*Solutions on page 41*]

1.2 Access to records

An individual field of a record may be referenced using a notation in which the identifier of the record is followed by a '.' (full stop) and then the field identifier. For example,

> *MyRecord.Name*

This is referred to this as the **dot notation** for record fields.

refers to the *Name* field of some record called *MyRecord*. So if *MyRecord* is a variable of type *MemberType* (defined on page 7), then *MyRecord.Name* is the identifier of a string variable whose value occupies the *Name* field of this record. As a result, *MyRecord.Name* can be manipulated using any of the operations that are appropriate to strings. In particular, assigning a value to a string is an allowable operation, so

> *MyRecord.Name* ← "John Smith"

will have the effect of assigning the string "John Smith" to the *Name* field of *MyRecord*. Similarly, the value of the *Age* field of this record would be incremented by 1 by the following assignment.

> *MyRecord.Age* ← *MyRecord.Age* + 1

The following design fragment writes out the telephone number on the record provided that the age of the associated member exceeds 30.

```
1    if MyRecord.Age > 30 then
2        write out MyRecord.TeleNo
3    ifend
```

There is nothing deep going on here. Just remember that a record is made up of a number of variables (its fields), each of which can be accessed by this dot notation. The fields can then be manipulated as normal variables. The following exercises provide you with practice in using this notation to access and manipulate fields.

Exercise 1.4

Suppose that *FJrec* is a variable of type *MemberType*. Write down a sequence of assignment steps to refine the design step

1   initialise *FJrec*

by supplying the information on a member called Frank Jones, whose address is 26 Lomaria Avenue, Oldtown. TN2 3ZN, who is male, 34 years old, and has telephone number 01987 654321.

Exercise 1.5

Suppose that *ArrowPos* is a variable of type *CursorPosType*, as described in the solution to Exercise 1.2. Suppose further that *ArrowPos* has been initialised. (It will therefore hold the row and column numbers of some position on the screen.)

(a) How do you refer to the row and column numbers of the position on the screen held by *ArrowPos*?

(b) Write design steps to move the position represented by *ArrowPos* one place upwards on the screen if it is not already at the top of the screen, and then one place to the right if it is not already on the extreme right.

(c) Write design steps which update *ArrowPos* so that it represents the position of the bottom left corner of the screen.

[*Solutions on page 42*]

In addition to various operations on each individual field of a record, there are a few operations that can be carried out on whole records. First there is record assignment. If *MyRecord* and *YourRecord* are two variables declared to be of the same record type, then (and only then) the assignment

> *YourRecord* ← *MyRecord*

is allowed. Its effect is to copy the value in each field of *MyRecord* to the corresponding field of *YourRecord*.

When the value of one record has been assigned to another, the two records have the same value in every field, and are said to be **equal**. The equality operator (and with it the 'not equal' operator) can be applied to records.

The other four comparison operators, $<, >, \geq$ and $\leq$ are not used with record structures.

Exercise 1.6 ―――――――――――――――――――――――――

The two record variables *HisRecord* and *HerRecord* are of the same type, but are different in type from *MyRecord* and *YourRecord*, which are of the same type. Which of the following design fragments are valid?

(a)   **if** *HisRecord = HerRecord* **then**
            YourRecord ← *MyRecord*
        ifend

(b)   **if** *MyRecord = YourRecord* **then**
            MyRecord ← *HisRecord*
        ifend

(c)   **if** *MyRecord < YourRecord* **then**
            HerRecord ← *HisRecord*
        ifend

(d)   **if** *HisRecord ≠ HerRecord* **then**
            MyRecord ← *YourRecord*
        ifend

[*Solution on page 43*]

―――――――――――――――――――――――――――――――――――――――

The previous exercise is about design concepts. As mentioned in the next section not all programming languages allow easy implementation of these design concepts.

1.3 Records in C++

Whereas the built-in types, such as integer and character, are always available for use anywhere in a C++ program, programmer-defined types given by **structure definitions** will be available only in programs, or parts of programs, where they have been defined. Just as with the index card template, the C++ compiler needs to be told the structure of a record—it needs a structure (type) definition.

In C++, the keyword **struct** is used to tell the compiler that a structure (or record) is about to be defined. For example, the type *MemberType* (see page 7) is defined by the following C++ statement.

```
struct  MemberType
{
 AnsiString  Name;
 AnsiString  Address;
 AnsiString  PostCode;
 char  Gender;
 int  Age;
 AnsiString  TeleNo;
};
```

The alignment of the types of the field identifiers is course style. The presence of the semicolon after the right brace is explained below.

This statement defines a record type with identifier *MemberType*, but as yet there are no variables of this type. To declare variables of this record type, you would make individual variable declarations. For example, the declaration of two variables of this type is as follows.

```
MemberType ABRec;
MemberType FJRec;
```

Alternatively, the two declarations could be *attached* to the structure definition as follows. Note that the variable identifiers are separated by a comma, and are followed by a semicolon. However, it will be course team style to *not* include variable declarations with the structure definition. They are logically separate actions and they will be written separately.

```
struct  MemberType
{
 AnsiString  Name;
 AnsiString  Address;
 AnsiString  PostCode;
 char  Gender;
 int  Age;
 AnsiString  TeleNo;
} ABRec, FJRec;    // not course style
```

The general form of the structure definition is as follows.

```
struct   TypeName
{
 type    FieldName1;
 type    FieldName2;
    ...
 type    FieldNameN;
};
```

The semicolon terminating the structure definition statement is essential; it must follow the right brace to indicate that there are no variable declarations included with the structure definition.

The declaration of variables of this type takes the following form.

```
TypeName Variable1;
TypeName Variable2;
   ...
TypeName VariableM;
```

Here *TypeName* is the identifier given to the structure. The fields of a record are accessed in C++ statements using the same 'dot notation' as was introduced at design. So, for example, *FJRec.Name* will be the identifier for the *Name* field in the *FJRec* record. If you understood manipulation of records at design stage, then you should have no problems with the corresponding code. All the key ideas are involved in the following exercise, which includes an opportunity for you to practise writing down a C++ structure definition.

Exercise 1.7 _____

A furniture warehouse stocks quantities of a number of items. A record system is maintained whereby, for each stocked item, the following information is stored:

o   an identification code in the form of a string;

o   the current stock level;

o   the unit cost of the item (in whole numbers of pounds);

o   the name of the supplier.

(a) Write down a C++ structure definition for these records, called *ItemType*, and declare, separately, three variables *SmallTable, NewTable* and *SoftSofa* of this type.

(b) Write a fragment of C++ code to initialise *SmallTable* to contain information on a new item with code TB56, stock level 50, selling at 299 pounds each and supplied by Tableland.

(c) Write a C++ statement to copy all the constituent values in the *SmallTable* to *NewTable*.

(d) Write a C++ statement to reduce the stock level of *SoftSofa* by 1.

(e) Write a fragment of C++ code which checks the stock level of *SoftSofa* and, if the level has fallen below 5, writes out an appropriate message saying that stock of the item with this code is getting low.

[*Solution on page 43*]

Some practical programming languages (PASCAL, for example) permit comparison of records. C++ does *not* permit comparison of **struct**s, even for equality. Thus, the only way of comparing two **struct**s for equality in C++ is by checking equality of corresponding members of each **struct**.

The record structure provides a way of holding together, under a single identifier, several items of information relating to one entity. In situations where records occur naturally, there is an additional problem: there will usually be large numbers of them. For instance, the warehouse of Exercise 1.7 might stock several hundred different items, and so several hundred variables of the type *ItemType* would be required. It would be tiresome if all the variables had to be declared individually:

```
ItemType Table1;
ItemType SmallTable;
ItemType NewTable;
   ...
ItemType SoftSofa;
```

The accompanying data table would have to describe each of the variables used.

not to mention the difficulty of trying to remember which variable represents which item of furniture.

As a more familiar example, consider a telephone directory. The natural structure for each entry in the directory is a record comprising three fields: a name, an address and a telephone number. The directory consists of many thousands of such records, and you certainly would not want to have to declare them individually. The telephone directory has an additional, crucial feature. The data within it is organised in an orderly fashion to help the user find required information. In designing programs that involve large numbers of records, the data must also be organised carefully. As a first step in that direction the next section brings the important notion of the **array** into play.

2 Arrays

The record, as introduced in the previous section, provides a way of dealing with related data of *different* types, as a whole. In this section, the main concern is with (potentially very large) numbers of items that are all of the *same* type.

2.1 Introducing arrays

The type *AnsiString*, introduced briefly in Block I, provides a most convenient representation of strings in which the string is built up as a sequence of characters. In addition to certain basic operations on whole strings, you can, by making use of an index, refer to and manipulate the individual characters in the string. The underlying idea used here, of forming a sequence of variables of the same type and bringing them together under a single identifier with an index, can be extended to any type at all, not just characters. Such indexed collections are called **arrays**.

As an example, consider a tennis club that runs a singles 'ladder competition' in which ten members participate. The ladder consists of an ordered list of players' names, as illustrated below.

Devlin
McCready
Peterson
Eldridge
McEldowney
Boyd
Stewart
McIlroy
Hylands
Gibson

Players may challenge the person immediately above them on the ladder; if the 'lower' person wins, their positions are interchanged. For example, Stewart may challenge Boyd, and if Stewart wins the ensuing match between them, then their positions on the ladder are switched. The underlying principle is that, when the ladder has been in operation for some time, the ordering of the players should reflect, more or less, their playing ability — with the best player at the top of the ladder and the worst at the bottom.

One way to store this information would be to use ten string variables with the following declarations.

```
AnsiString Pos1;
AnsiString Pos2;
AnsiString Pos3;
AnsiString Pos4;
AnsiString Pos5;
AnsiString Pos6;
AnsiString Pos7;
AnsiString Pos8;
AnsiString Pos9;
AnsiString Pos10;
```

and to assign the name at the top of the ladder to *Pos1*, the next name to *Pos2*, and so on. The values of these variables could then be reassigned as players change position on the ladder.

Whilst this approach is quite feasible for a ladder of ten names, it is already looking a little clumsy. If the club were to extend the ladder to twenty players, manipulation of twenty string variables would be required! It also has the fault that the way the data is stored does not really reflect the fact that the variables are part of the ladder entity. An alternative approach that accommodates a ladder of any size, and provides a way of

referring to the whole ladder is to use an **array**, with an index, by means
of which the elements of the array are indexed, as shown below.

Ladder

0	Devlin
1	McCready
2	Peterson
3	Eldridge
4	McEldowney
5	Boyd
6	Stewart
7	McIlroy
8	Hylands
9	Gibson

The whole ladder is referred to by the single identifier *Ladder*, and its ten
elements (each of type string) are indexed from 0 to 9. So, for example,
Ladder[0] and *Ladder*[7] are the identifiers of string variables whose current
values are "Devlin" and "McIlroy", respectively.

In general, the elements of any array must be of the same type, and fixed in number.

You may be wondering why the indexing is from 0 to 9, rather than the
more natural 1 to 10: it is a C++ requirement.

In C++, arrays are always indexed beginning at 0.

This contrasts with the indexing of a string, which starts at 1.

Most programming languages do allow the programmer to specify any
index range. However, C++ has reasons for forcing the index range always
to start at 0. Whilst, as in this ladder example, it might be more
convenient to choose a different index range, the course team decided to
bear with the C++ constraint and design all arrays to start at index 0. (If
you ever work with a language that permits more freedom, then it may
make your code more readable to choose other ranges when appropriate.)

In addition to its identifier, *Ladder*, there are two key features that
determine the array structure. They are the type of each of its
elements — and remember that in an array all the elements must be of the
same type — and the number of elements. The data table entry that
captures these attributes is as follows.

Type	Identifier	Description
Array of string	*Ladder*[10]	An array holding names

The identifier is *Ladder*; [10] is an 'attachment', as discussed below.

In C++, the declaration of this array is

```
AnsiString Ladder[10];
```

The C++ declaration does not involve any keywords telling us that it is an
array structure; that information is embodied in the fact that the given
identifier is indexed. As always, the declaration begins with the type
involved, here *AnsiString*. For arrays, the declared type is that of its
constituent elements and is referred to as the **base type** of the array. Next
comes the identifier *Ladder*, and because *Ladder* has the attachment '[10]'
it is interpreted as an array with ten elements of the base type (which here
is *AnsiString*). The ten elements will be indexed from 0 to 9 inclusive.

As a further example, the declaration

```
float Prices[25];
```

declares an array, with identifier *Prices*, of 25 real numbers (since the base type is **float**). As indexing always begins at 0, the 25 elements are indexed from 0 to 24 and consequently the 25 values have references *Prices*[0], *Prices*[1], ..., *Prices*[24].

The individual elements of an array are variables of the base type. For example, *Ladder*[5] is a string variable. All the usual string operations are available to be applied to *Ladder*[5]. In particular, once *Ladder* has been declared, a value, "Stewart" say, can be assigned to this element of the array by means of the standard C++ assignment statement.

```
Ladder[5] = "Stewart";
```

The base type of an array does not have to be one of the built-in types; it can be any type at all, including programmer-defined types. In the tennis club example, an array could be created consisting of records of the structured type *MemberType* by means of the declaration

```
MemberType Club[300];
```

This declaration assumes that the structure definition for *MemberType* has been made previously.

that sets up an array, called *Club*, which holds 300 records at indexes 0 to 299.

Exercise 2.1

(a) Write down the C++ declaration of the array *Count* of base type integer which comprises 100 elements.

(b) Explain what *Count*[27] is.

Exercise 2.2

For each of the following parts, write down a C++ variable declaration to declare an array to hold the information referred to.

(a) The six whole numbers (from 1 to 49 inclusive) held by a person as their entry in the National Lottery.

(b) The air temperature recorded at midday at a certain weather station for each day during 1997.

(c) A football league table recording, for each of 18 teams, the team name together with the number of matches played, won, drawn and lost and the current points total. (You will need to make a structure definition first.)

Exercise 2.3

Write a sequence of design steps to swap the elements at indexes 5 and 6 of the array *Ladder*. Be careful!

[Solutions on page 44]

2.2 Operations on arrays

An array must possess the following two properties:

o it consists of a fixed number of elements;

o the elements are all of the same base type.

The two attributes identified here, namely the size of the array and the base type, are what are needed (along with a chosen identifier) to specify the array. The base type can be any defined type, either one of the built-in types or a programmer-defined type. You have seen examples of arrays of records and, in due course, you will meet an array of arrays.

The size of the array not only specifies how many elements there are, it also pins down the precise index range of the array. If the size is stipulated as N, then, since arrays are always indexed from 0 in C++, there are N elements occupying indexes $0, 1, 2, \ldots, N - 1$.

The type *AnsiString* was used to introduce the idea of arrays, drawing on the analogy with an indexed sequence of characters. But it must be pointed out that *AnsiString* is not in fact an array type; it is something quite different, as you will see later in this block. For the time being, note that an *AnsiString* variable differs from an array of characters in two major respects. First, it does not have a fixed size: you do not have to specify how long your string is to be when you declare it. Secondly, indexing of a string variable begins at 1: the first character (if any) in the string is found at index 1.

There is a limit of about 2 billion characters on how large an *AnsiString* variable may become. It takes up only the memory actually needed at any one time.

For each of the other types and structures that have been introduced, the question of what operations are supported has always been asked. In the case of arrays, the answer is easy. There are *no* operations directly on whole arrays. Information held in an array, such as *Ladder*, can be stored, manipulated and retrieved by accessing individual elements, such as *Ladder*[3], through use of the index.

One implication of the statement that there are no operations directly on whole arrays is that array assignment is not allowed. Even if *MyArray* and *YourArray* are declared to be of the same size and same base type, and are both initialised, the attempted assignment

```
YourArray = MyArray;          // illegal
```

is not allowed in C++. Indeed, you might expect the statement

```
YourArray = 0;          // illegal
```

to initialise all elements of the array to 0. This is not so; again because assignment is not a permitted operation on arrays.

The values of one array can be assigned to those of another, but this must be done element by element.

Likewise, there are no comparison operations. So, no matter how much you are tempted to compare arrays by means of a statement such as

```
if (MyArray == YourArray)          // illegal comparison
  statement;
```

you cannot do so.

Two arrays with the same size N and the same base type are **equal** when each of the N pairs of corresponding elements are equal. Thus two arrays, of the same size and type, can be compared for equality only by comparing each pair of corresponding elements for equality.

The following exercise explores these ideas.

Exercise 2.4 _____

Suppose that *MyArray* and *YourArray* are arrays of base type integer, each holding 10 elements. Suppose further that both arrays have been initialised.

(a) Write a design fragment to update the value of *YourArray* so that it is equal to *MyArray*. (You should use a **while** loop to copy the element values in turn.)

(b) Write a design fragment whose purpose is to assign to a boolean variable *Equals* the value true if *YourArray* is equal to *MyArray*, and assign value false otherwise. (As in part (a), a **while** loop is required.)

[*Solution on page 45*]

_____

You may be wondering why there is such emphasis on specifying which operations are allowed, and which are not, on the various data types you meet. The need to encapsulate types of data and the operations which manipulate that data has grown in importance as computing languages have developed. Originally, programming languages provided just basic types — such as integer, real and character — together with ways of building from them, like the array. If the programmer needed any non-standard operations on a created type, the code to support the operation had to be written. If a different program required use of the same type, it would be inefficient to have to remake the structure definition, along with all the code to support operations on it. The desirability of reusing data types and the realisation that the operations and data formed a logical whole is part of the reason for the development of **objects**, which you will meet later in this block.

For the time being, you will have to keep track of what operations are allowed on the various types. In the case of arrays, everything has to be done by manipulation of the individual elements, which are accessed by means of the array index.

2.3 Tables

Records are rarely used singly; they almost invariably occur in collections of records of the same type. For example, in the tennis club example of Section 1, the record type *MemberType* was created to hold information about individual members. The secretary would have to maintain a collection of such records.

There are various ways by which users can collate records into larger structures. One such is an 'array of records'. A key feature of an array is that all its constituent elements must be of the same type, but there is no reason why this 'same' type should not be structured (i.e. programmer-defined). An array of records is called a **table**.

For example, in the declaration
`MemberType Club[300]`
of Subsection 2.1, *MemberType* is a programmer-defined type.

Everyday life presents many examples of tables. Daily newspapers, for instance, publish tables of currency exchange rates, as illustrated below. (This table was for late 2001 and does not take into account the switch to the Euro.)

Exchange

Index	Country	Currency	Rate
0	Austria	Schilling	21.95
1	Belgium	Franc	64.37
2	Canada	Dollar	2.29
3	Holland	Guilder	3.52
4	France	Franc	10.46
5	Germany	Mark	3.12
6	Ireland	Punt	1.27
7	Italy	Lire	3089.00
8	Japan	Yen	175.40
9	Portugal	Escudo	319.91
10	Spain	Peseta	265.51
11	United States	Dollar	1.59

Each entry in this table is a record with three fields: the name of the country, the name of the currency and its exchange rate (giving the equivalent of 1 pound sterling). This table is called *Exchange* and, to emphasise that the natural structure for this table is an array, the index numbers of the entries are written in the left-hand column. The declaration of *Exchange* in C++ is as follows.

```
struct  RateRecordType
{
 AnsiString  Country;
 AnsiString  Currency;
 float  Rate;
};
RateRecordType Exchange[12];
```

This declares *Exchange* to be an array with 12 elements (indexed from 0 to 11), where each element is of type *RateRecordType*. The record *Exchange*[0] holds information about the Austrian currency, *Exchange*[1] holds information about the Belgian currency, and so on. *Exchange*[7].*Country* is a string variable holding the value of the *Country* field in record *Exchange*[7]. The value of *Exchange*[7].*Country* is Italy. Other fields are referred to in the same way.

Exercise 2.5 _____

Suppose that *Exchange* has been initialised as in the table above. Write down variable identifiers whose values are:

(a) the name of the Portuguese currency;

(b) the exchange rate with Canada;

(c) the whole record of information about Germany.

[*Solution on page 45*]

_____

It is difficult to overstate the importance of tables. Vast quantities of data are stored in tables, usually called **databases**, and manipulated for all sorts of purposes. A large proportion of code that is written and maintained for non-embedded computer systems is for database purposes, and so deals with tables. Much of the code library supplied with Builder is for such purposes.

2.4 Two-dimensional arrays

By now you should be beginning to appreciate the usefulness of the array construction. However, up to this point, all arrays have been one-dimensional. That is, the elements of the array are accessed by a single index. But there are many problems in which the data is represented naturally as an array of arrays: a **two-dimensional array**. (The table of the previous subsection may appear two-dimensional but it is a one-dimensional array of records.) For example, consider the layout of characters on a printed page of text. The page may comprise 40 lines, each containing 80 characters (many of which will be the space character). The page may be thought of as a 40×80 array of characters.

The C^{++} language allows multi-dimensional arrays, though this course will not require anything beyond the second dimension.

At design, this array might be created by the following data table entry.

Type	Identifier	Description
Array of character	*Page*[40][80]	2-dimensional array of characters

The corresponding declaration in C^{++} would be

```
char Page[40][80];
```

One convenient way of thinking of this is as an array of arrays. It is an array of size 40 with base type array of size 80 with (in turn) base type character. Remembering that C^{++} always begins array indexes at 0, you can visualise the 3200 constituent character variables making up *Page* as follows:

Page[0][0]	*Page*[0][1]	*Page*[0][2]	...	*Page*[0][79]
Page[1][0]	*Page*[1][1]	*Page*[1][2]	...	*Page*[1][79]
Page[2][0]	*Page*[2][1]	*Page*[2][2]	...	*Page*[2][79]
⋮	⋮	⋮	⋮	⋮
Page[39][0]	*Page*[39][1]	*Page*[39][2]	...	*Page*[39][79]

Observe that each entry of the array is identified by a pair of indexes; it takes the form

$Page[Row][Column]$

where the first index, called *Row*, can take any value in the range from 0 to 39, and the second index, *Column*, can take any value in the range from 0 to 79.

Note that each index is held in its own pair of square brackets. (Some languages allow you to write

```
Page[Row, Column]    // illegal in C++
```

but C++ does not.)

The array *Page* could have been declared with its indexes in reverse order:

```
char Page[80][40];
```

Had this been the case, the individual elements in *Page* would be accessed by

$Page[Column][Row]$

Once the array declaration has been made, the order of the indexes is fixed.

In general, the declaration of a two-dimensional array takes the following form.

```
BaseType   ArrayName[FirstIndexSize][SecondIndexSize];
```

This creates (*FirstIndexSize*) × (*SecondIndexSize*) variables of type *BaseType* which have identifiers of the form

```
ArrayName[FirstIndex][SecondIndex]
```

The following exercise tests your basic understanding of the two-dimensional array structure and how to access its elements. (Later in this block, you will meet and use more ambitious examples of arrays.)

Exercise 2.6 _____

The table below holds the four assignment grades, as percentages, of 350 students on a (fictitious) Open University course. Each row represents the performance of one student. Assignments 1, 2, 3 and 4, occupy respectively the first, second, third and fourth columns of the table. Each student has a number in the range 1 to 350, the performance of student number 1 being in the first row, that of student number 2 in the second row, and so on.

67	78	69	54
36	65	29	51
34	52	98	17
34	...	...	...
⋮	⋮	⋮	⋮
67	86	87	91

(a) Give a C++ declaration for a two-dimensional array of integers, called *AGrades*, to hold this information.

(b) Suppose the array has been initialised.

  (i) Write down a C++ expression whose value is the grade that student number 57 obtained on Assignment 3.

  (ii) Write a fragment of C++ code (including initialisation and declaration of variables, as required) to determine the mean grade for student number 37.

[*Solution on page 46*]

3 For loops

Most high-level programming languages provide the equivalent of the **while** loop, although it is sometimes heavily disguised. It is possible to use **while** loops for any situation where a loop is required. However, designs and code are often more readable if other forms of loop are available. For example, the **when** loop, which you used in *Unit 3* of Block I, may require fewer initialisations.

Useful operations on arrays, such as comparing them or copying one to another, can be achieved only on an element-by-element basis. A basic operation has to be repeated for each element of the array or arrays. It is perfectly possible to use **while** loops for such purposes, but because the size of array (number of repeats) is known in advance, another form of loop — the **for loop** — is particularly useful in this setting. The potential of such loops is explored in this section.

The **for** loop was mentioned briefly in *Unit 3*, Block I.

3.1 Unconditioned loops

Suppose that you are confronted with the task of initialising the array *Ladder* to consist of ten names. The following design, in which the loop control is governed by the integer variable *Index*, gets the user to enter the names from the keyboard.

```
1    Index ← 0
2    loop while Index ≤ 9
3        write out "Enter next name: "
4        read in Ladder[Index]
5        Index ← Index + 1
6    loopend
```

Here the loop body is executed a fixed number of times, namely 10, which is known in advance. The above design to initialise *Ladder*, can be rewritten as a **for** loop, as below. The use of a **for** loop makes the fixed number of repetitions more obvious.

```
1    loop for Index ← 0 to 9
2        write out "Enter next name: "
3        read in Ladder[Index]
4    loopend
```

This **for** loop does not appear to have a step initialising the control variable *Index*, and no step incrementing *Index* at each pass of the loop. In fact, the loop statement, step 1, takes care of both of these aspects. It tells us that *Index* is initialised to 0, incremented by 1 at each pass, and iteration is terminated when *Index* exceeds 9.

The assignment arrow is used in step 1 because in that step *Index* is assigned the values 0, 1, ..., 9, one after the other.

The fact that incrementation is by 1 is the default option. The loop control variable can increment in steps other than 1, in which case a step value would be specified in the control statement. For example, the body of the loop

> **loop for** *Index* ← 1 **to** 10 **step** 2

The *body* of the loop comprises the steps between the **loop for** control step and the **loopend**.

would execute first with *Index* = 1 and subsequently with *Index* = 3, 5, 7 and 9. *Index* would then be incremented to a value that exceeds the top limit in the control statement, and so iteration would terminate.

The increment step could be negative, in which case the control variable counts down from its initial value, in the appropriate steps, until it is less than the second value. For example,

> **loop for** *Count* ← 10 **to** 1 **step** −1

is controlled by an integer variable *Count* which starts at 10 and reduces by 1 following each iteration of the loop down to the final iteration during which *Count* has value 1.

Exercise 3.1

What will be output when the following **for** loop is executed, where *Index* is an integer variable?

```
1    loop for Index ← −6 to 6 step 3
2        write out Index * (Index + 1)
3    loopend
```

23

Exercise 3.2 _____

Suppose that *MyReals* is an array consisting of 25 real numbers.

(a) Write a design which uses a **for** loop to enter value 0 at each of the 25 elements of *MyReals*.

(b) Write a design which uses a **for** loop to initialise *MyReals* with values which are read in, in index order, from the keyboard.

[*Solutions on page 46*]

Before turning to the implementation of the **for** loop, you need to be aware of one common error in its use. Remember that the loop control step looks after incrementation of the control variable, so

Never change the value of the control variable inside the **for** loop body.

For example, in the following code you might have accidentally included the step which increments the control variable inside the loop body, or indeed you might have done so deliberately, in the hope that it would result in the design fragment writing out alternate elements in *Ladder*.

```
1     loop for Index ← 0 to 9
2         write out Ladder[Index]
3             Index ← Index + 1
4     loopend
```

While the control step 1 increments *Index* in steps of 1, step 3 is attempting to accelerate the incrementation. How will *Index* vary here? The answer is that the outcome of executing this design is unpredictable and depends on the language being used and the particular implementation. The message is that you must never change the value of a **for** loop control variable inside the loop body. Whatever you attempt to achieve by it can always be managed in some other, unambiguous, way.

3.2 For loops in C++

The general form of the C++ **for** statement is

```
for (initialisation; condition; increment)
   {single or compound statement}
```

In its most common usage the *initialisation* is an assignment statement that sets the initial value of the loop control variable, the *condition* is a condition which determines whether iteration of the loop continues or stops, and *increment* determines the step by which the control variable changes each time the loop is repeated. These three major sections of the control statement must be separated by semicolons. If the statement in the loop body is a single statement, the braces may be omitted. Each statement in the loop body must end with a semicolon.

The loop body is executed repeatedly as long as the condition remains true. Once the condition becomes false, the program execution resumes with the statement following the **for** statement.

Here are two examples of **for** loops in C++.

Example 3.1

The array *Ladder* can be initialised by the following statement, in which the integer variable *Index* controls a **for** loop.

```
int Index;  // The control variable must be declared.
 for (Index = 0; Index < 10; Index = Index + 1)
 {
  WriteIntPr("Enter name for position  ", Index);
  Ladder[Index] = ReadString();
 }
```

The loop is executed with *Index* running through the values from 0 to 9 respectively (in steps of 1) and, for each value, the name at this position is read in following an appropriate prompt. □

Example 3.2

The following code fragment counts how many times the letter 'A' occurs in a string which is entered from the keyboard. The integer variable *ACount* is used to count the A's, *I* is the loop control variable, and the string variable *InString* holds the input string. These three variables would have to be declared in the code preceding the fragment.

```
InString = ReadStringPr("Enter a string: ");
ACount = 0;
for (I = 1; I <= Length(InString); I = I + 1)
{
 if (InString[I] == 'A')
   ACount = ACount + 1;
}
WriteIntPr("The number of A's in the string is  ", ACount);
```

Although the use of meaningful identifiers for variables has been encouraged, the use of a single letter, particularly *I* or *J*, as the loop control variable of a **for** loop is quite common in the literature.

In this example the **for** loop body is enclosed in braces, but the braces are not essential since the loop body consists of just a single statement, namely the **if** statement. The loop control sets the variable *I* to range over the consecutive values from 1 to *Length(InString)*, and thus *InString[I]* takes the value of each of the characters in *InString* in turn. Each time an 'A' is encountered one is added to *ACount*. □

As with other constructs, there is no harm done by including the unnecessary braces. If it helps you to appreciate the program structure, then include them.

Exercise 3.3 _____

Determine what each of the following code fragments achieves. The array *Ladder* was declared in Subsection 2.1.

(a)
```
   int Index;
   for (Index = 0; Index < 10; Index = Index + 2)
    WriteStringCr(Ladder[Index]);
```

(b)
```
   int Index;
   for (Index = 10; Index >= 7; Index = Index - 1)
   {
    WriteInt(Index);
    WriteChar(' ');
    WriteIntCr(Index * Index);
   }
```

(c) In this part, it might help you to trace through the code using the surnames of the array *Ladder*, given on page 15.

```
int Index;
int First;
 First = 0;
  for (Index = 1; Index < 10 ; Index = Index + 1)
    if (Ladder[Index] < Ladder[First])
      First = Index;        // Note that the for loop body ends here.
  WriteString(Ladder[First]);
```

Exercise 3.4

Write fragments of C++ code, in each case using a **for** loop, to carry out each of the following tasks.

(a) Write out the reciprocal of each of the whole numbers from 1 to 20 inclusive, in the following form.

> The reciprocal of a non-zero number x is $1/x$.

```
    1   1.000000
    2   0.500000
    etc.
```

(b) Write out the elements at the odd numbered indexes in array *Ladder*, of size 10, in reverse order (on separate lines).

[Solutions on page 47]

You should note that C++ allows the **for** loop to be used with much more versatility than these examples suggest. The C++ **for** loop is really a shorthand way of coding a particular form of **while** loop. Rather than having one loop control variable, **for** loops can be designed with two, three, and even zero control variables. Control conditions can be much more complex than simple tests on the value of the control variable. In this course, however, **for** loops will be restricted to the situations for which they were originally designed, namely when the number of iterations is known, exactly, in advance. This restriction is in line with their use in some other languages where the C++ extended forms are not available.

> There are (almost unreadable) examples of code where the entire processing takes place inside the loop condition and increment statements. This is one way to ensure that no one else can maintain your code!

3.3 A problem involving arrays

To round off this section you will work through a complete problem, with guidance, reaching a design solution and then coding it.

Problem Specification   Examination Grades

Each student sitting an examination has been awarded one of the grades $0, 1, 2, \ldots, 10$ to indicate the level of performance obtained. The examination board has requested some analysis of these results; to be precise, they would like to know, for each of the eleven possible grades, how many students obtained this grade and what percentage of the total number of examinees this represents. The list of student grades currently exists on paper, and the requirement is for a program in which the grades are entered from the keyboard, and the requested analysis is output to the screen.   □

Is it clear what is required? There is no indication of how many examinees there are, although this information will be inherent in the list of student grades. As with the 'mean' problem that you tackled in *Unit 2*, Block I, some way is needed of indicating when the end of input has been reached: an appropriate sentinel value. Hopefully the specification has provided all other information that is required, so solution design can be started.

As each grade is input, it can be processed by updating counts (of grades), and then discarded as the next one is read in. So there is no need to store all the grades; thus the following top-level design should fit the bill.

1   initialise counts
2   **loop while** there are more grades to input
3   read in and process next grade
4   **loopend**
5   write out results

How is the data to be handled? Grades (as integers in the range 0 to 10) are to be entered from the keyboard, and you need to count how many of each there are. So eleven variables, one for each of the counts, will be needed, and the sensible way to organise these variables is as a single array with eleven elements.

Exercise 3.5 ⎯⎯⎯⎯⎯⎯⎯⎯

Give the Type column entry of the data table for the array, called *Frequency*, that will be needed to hold the eleven counts. Give a C++ declaration of this array.

[*Solution on page 48*]

The eleven elements of *Frequency* are going to be used for the eleven counts; for example, *Frequency*[3] is the identifier of an integer variable used to count how many grades of 3 are entered from the keyboard. Each of these elements must be initialised to 0 as part of step 1. A **for** loop is ideal for this purpose.

1.1 **loop for** $I \leftarrow 0$ **to** 10
1.2 $Frequency[I] \leftarrow 0$
1.3 **loopend**

Variable I will have to be
added to the data table.

There may well be other variables to be initialised in step 1. One such
variable can be anticipated. As the specification asks for the percentage of
students scoring each grade, you are going to have to know how many
grades in total are entered. An integer variable called *CountOfGrades* will
be used for this purpose. This count must also be started at 0, so another
step in the refinement of step 1 is required.

It is not essential to count the
number of grades as they are
entered. This could be
achieved by totalling the
eleven frequencies.

1.4 $CountOfGrades \leftarrow 0$

Now consider the processing loop. Numbers are to be read from the
keyboard, so an integer variable *Grade*, say, will be needed for the input.
Each grade will be recorded by incrementing the appropriate element of
Frequency. For example, when a 7 is entered, *Frequency*[7] is incremented
by 1. It is not known how many numbers there are going to be, so a
conditioned loop is appropriate. As suggested above, a sentinel value will
be used to indicate that input has finished; that is, when the final actual
grade has been entered, a value not in the range 0 to 10 is then used to
terminate input.

Exercise 3.6

Refine steps 2 and 3 using a conditioned loop with 999 as a sentinel value.

[Solution on page 48]

When this processing loop is completed, the elements of *Frequency* hold the
required totals for each of the eleven grades and *CountOfGrades* holds the
final count of the number of grades entered. Step 5 requires that all eleven
values of *Frequency* are written out, each accompanied by what percentage
of the total this represents. Once again, a **for** loop is the natural way
forward. The following refinement of step 5 introduces the real variable
Percentage for holding, temporarily, the result of the percentage calculation
for each grade.

5.1 **loop for** $I \leftarrow 0$ **to** 10
5.2   write out "For grade ", I
5.3   write out ", Frequency = ", $Frequency[I]$
5.4 $Percentage \leftarrow Frequency[I] * 100 / CountOfGrades$
5.5   write out " and Percentage = ", $Percentage$
5.6 **loopend**

The design is just about complete, but before putting it all together a data
table is required which shows all the variables that have been introduced.

Type	Identifier	Description
Array of integer	$Frequency[11]$	Array holding counts of each grade
Integer	I	Control variable for **for** loops
Integer	$CountOfGrades$	Count of total number of grades
Integer	$Grade$	Grade entered from keyboard; range is 0 to 10 with sentinel 999
Real	$Percentage$	Percentage of each grade

Here is the complete design.

1.1 **loop for** $I \leftarrow 0$ **to** 10
1.2 $Frequency[I] \leftarrow 0$
1.3 **loopend**
1.4 $CountOfGrades \leftarrow 0$
2.1 write out "Enter first grade: "
2.2 read in $Grade$
2.3 **loop while** $Grade \neq 999$
3.1 $CountOfGrades \leftarrow CountOfGrades + 1$
3.2 $Frequency[Grade] \leftarrow Frequency[Grade] + 1$
3.3   write out "Enter next grade or 999 to terminate: "
3.4   read in $Grade$
4 **loopend**
5.1 **loop for** $I \leftarrow 0$ **to** 10
5.2   write out "For grade ", I
5.3   write out ", Frequency = ", $Frequency[I]$
5.4 $Percentage \leftarrow Frequency[I] * 100 / CountOfGrades$
5.5   write out " and Percentage = ", $Percentage$
5.6 **loopend**

Having reached a design that is ready for coding, you should always reflect on what has been achieved before proceeding further. Are you happy with the design solution? In fact, it will solve the problem as specified; but, as so often happens with programs like this one, there are still potential difficulties associated with wrongly entered data. The solution will not cater for the user making a mistake at the keyboard. If the user accidentally entered a grade of 22, the program would suffer a run-time error when an attempt is made to reference the non-existent variable $Frequency[22]$.

The operating system would object to accessing memory that did not belong to the *Frequency* array.

As mentioned in *Unit 4* of Block I, these matters will not be discussed in any depth until more work has been done with user interfaces in Block III. For the time being, however, some range checking could be built into the design. The permitted keyboard entries are whole numbers in the range 0 to 10, or the sentinel value 999, so step 3.4 could be replaced by the following steps.

3.4.1 read in $Grade$
3.4.2 **loop while** $(Grade \neq 999)$ **and** $((Grade < 0)$ **or** $(Grade > 10))$
3.4.3   write out "Invalid number. Please enter again: "
3.4.4   read in $Grade$
3.4.5 **loopend**

This is similar to the range check incorporated into the solution of the problem First Word in *Unit 3*, Block I.

Testing the program should also reveal that the *division by zero* error is still a potential hazard. Action is needed to prevent the user terminating input before any grades have been entered. Better still, the user could be prevented from keying 999 in as the first entry.

Exercise 3.7 _____

Suggest a refinement for step 2.2 which will remove the division by zero difficulty.

[_Solution on page 49_]

With the suggested improvements, you can feel reasonably confident that the program will work correctly provided that the user enters whole numbers in response to the prompts. The design still does not cater for an entry which is not in the form of an integer.

3.4 Implementing the solution

To complete your solution to the Examination Grades problem, you need to code it, run it and test it. Before switching on your computer, you should at least map out, if not write out in full, your coded version of the design that has been reached. (The course team program includes the suggested refinements of steps 2.2 and 3.4.) Do not forget that you will have to include variable declarations for each entry in the data table, and that includes one for the array _Frequency_.

This is to be your first practical activity in Block II. The course team software for this block is all to be found in the **Block II** subfolder of MT262, and you should save all your work in this folder for the duration of this block. The MT262io library has been copied to the **Block II** folder.

Computer Activity 3.1 _____

o   Start Builder and open a new console application.

o   Before going any further, save the project by choosing **Save Project As...** from the **File** menu. Make sure that the active folder displayed in the **Save in** box is the **Block II** subfolder of MT262. Use the names **GradesU** for the unit file and **Grades** for the project file. (You _must_ make sure that **Block II**, not **Block I**, is selected for the **Save in** box of the **Save Project As** dialog box.)

o   Carry out the usual tasks to make the library MT262io available to your program and for holding the screen output.

o   Enter your code in the designated place in the file. When you are happy with your coding, attempt to run the program.

If you need a reminder on how to do this, check in the Handbook.

o   Correct any compilation errors that are revealed. When the program runs successfully, test it by using a variety of sample data.

[_Solution on page 53_]

4 Searching tables

Many applications of computers involve searching for a particular piece of information from a collection stored in the computer. A related idea is that of sorting (arranging) information into an order which is helpful for the use to which the data will be put. These two activities — searching and sorting — are closely related, in that suitable sorting of data can make the search process more efficient.

This course devotes rather less time than is usual in many other courses to searching and sorting, important though these topics are. The main reason is that the toolkit supplied with Builder has reusable code that deals with searching and sorting tables (and other data) and requires very little effort on the part of the programmer. The reason that *any* time is devoted to these topics is that such toolkits are not a standard part of C^{++}, even if they should be! You may be placed in a position where you are faced with the design and code of algorithms for sorts and searches, so you need some appreciation of the problems. It is also an area where *efficiency* is vital. An algorithm that sorts a few, or a few hundred, data items is not difficult to design. One that will sort tens or hundreds of thousands in a reasonable time is much more challenging.

4.1 Searching and sorting

Information in databases is often held in tables, or in structures similar to tables. To support such structures one would like to have available methods such as the following.

o Retrieve information from a record.

o Update information on a record.

o Delete a record.

o Insert a new record.

All of these will involve **searching**. To update or retrieve information from a record, or to delete that record, the correct record in the table must first be found. To insert a record, the correct position for insertion must be found.

How to approach searching a table depends heavily on just how the data in the table is organised. On page 19, a table of currency exchange rates was given; it was **sorted** by alphabetical ordering of the country name. In designing an algorithm to search this table for a given country name, it ought to be possible to capitalise on the fact that the field on which the search is done is sorted. As an illustration, compare the task of finding a given word in a dictionary. You would not start at page 1 of the dictionary and read each word until you find the one you are looking for! Knowing that the words are in alphabetical order, you can search much more efficiently.

On the other hand, the *Rate* field of the exchange table is unsorted. If asked to design an algorithm to search this table for a given exchange rate, you would struggle to do better than start with the first entry and look at each rate in turn until you find the wanted one, or reach the bottom of the table and conclude that the wanted rate is not there. If you found yourself searching this table more often for a given exchange rate than for a given country name, you might reorganise the entries in the table in order of increasing (or decreasing) exchange rate.

Searching and sorting are fundamental tasks to be carried out on data, and the task of designing efficient algorithms for these purposes has been an ongoing challenge to programmers for some time. When confronted with a table with 12 entries, say, you would quite reasonably dismiss efficiency as being irrelevant; with the speed of today's computers, you probably would fail to notice any difference between an efficient algorithm and an unimaginative search of the whole table from beginning to end. But databases do get very large, and then efficiency of algorithms does become a very important consideration in design.

The Open University's database of student records currently contains over 150 000 entries, quite enough to show up inefficient algorithms.

You are not going to become involved in any detailed study of sorting and searching algorithms in this course. However, to impart a little of the flavour, you are asked to look at two such algorithms in this section: a simple search algorithm (the 'linear search') and an efficient sorting algorithm.

4.2 The linear search

A **linear search** of an array or table (an array of records) involves starting at the first element and working through the array checking each entry in turn looking for a wanted value. As an example, the following illustrates part of a table holding information on train departures from a certain station for a particular day. For each train there is a departure time, a destination and a platform number.

Alternatively, the search could begin at the last element and work forwards through the array.

Time	Destination	Platform
...	...	...
...	...	...
06.25	Blackpool	3
06.30	Preston	2
06.48	Lytham	3
06.55	Bolton	4
07.00	Blackpool	3
07.03	Edinburgh	1
...	...	...
...	...	...

Suppose that the table is implemented in C++ by the following definitions.

```
struct TrainType
{
  AnsiString  Time;
  AnsiString  Destination;
  int Platform;
};
TrainType TimeTable[200];
int LastTrainIndex;
```

This declares *TimeTable* to be an array of 200 records, each with three fields. The integer variable *LastTrainIndex* holds the index of the final entry of the table, so information is held at indexes from 0 up to and including *LastTrainIndex*, which cannot exceed 199.

The table is ordered on the *Time* field, and it will be assumed that the entries in this field are unique, so that two trains cannot depart at the same time.

The scene is now set to search this table for various bits of information.

Example 4.1

Write a design whose purpose is to write out a list giving the departure times of all trains to Blackpool.

The search will involve scanning the *Destination* field of every entry in the table, and whenever the value "Blackpool" is encountered, the entry in the *Time* field of this same record has to be written out. Since all the entries in the timetable are to be searched and since there is a fixed number of entries, a **for** loop appears to be involved. A top-level design is as follows.

```
1    initialise variables
2    loop for all entries in timetable
3        process next entry
4    loopend
```

The processing in step 3 involves checking the *Destination* field of the current record and, if it is "Blackpool", writing out the entry in the *Time* field. This leads to the following refinement, in which the loop control variable *Index* covers the entire range from 0 to *LastTrainIndex*. (As the **for** loop takes care of its own initialisation, step 1 is not needed in this design.)

```
2.1    loop for Index ← 0 to LastTrainIndex
3.1        if TimeTable[Index].Destination = "Blackpool" then
3.2            write out TimeTable[Index].Time
3.3        ifend
4      loopend
```

The design searches one field of the collection of all records, but writes out information from a different field. For each value of *Index*, *TimeTable[Index].Destination* and *TimeTable[Index].Time* are associated values holding the destination and departure time of one particular train. □

Exercise 4.1 ⎯⎯⎯⎯⎯⎯⎯⎯⎯

Adapt the above design so that, instead of searching for trains to Blackpool, it searches for trains to any destination *PlaceWanted*, the latter being input by the user from the keyboard. Translate your design into a fragment of C++ code.

[*Solution on page 49*]

⎯⎯⎯⎯⎯⎯⎯⎯⎯⎯⎯⎯⎯⎯⎯⎯⎯⎯⎯⎯

If you are asked for information on just one record, rather than all records with a certain property, the search can halt on finding a *match* instead of continuing to the end of the table. To implement such searches it is better to use a **while** loop with an appropriate terminating condition, as illustrated in the next example.

You have seen in Subsection 3.1 of *Unit 3*, Block I that string values have an ordering. The times displayed in the table are in increasing string order, which agrees with increasing time order.

Although *LastTrainIndex* is a variable, its current value can be used in loop control, as here.

33

Example 4.2

Write a design whose purpose is to determine and write out the departure time and platform of the first train to Blackpool after 09.00.

The basic idea in the design will be to carry out a linear search again, starting at the first record and inspecting each record in turn until the first one with the required properties is found. The design given below makes essential use of the fact that the table is sorted on its *Time* field. At the start, the table is searched for the first record in which the value in the *Time* field is after 09.00. Once this record is located, the table is searched from this point for the first record which has value "Blackpool" in the *Destination* field. Since the search is going to break into two distinct phases, the following is a suitable top-level design.

Of course, the first record in which the value of *Time* is after 09.00 may well have "Blackpool" as the value of *Destination*, in which case the search stops there.

1 initialise variables
2 find index of first record with departure time after 09.00
3 search from index found for first record with destination "Blackpool"
4 write out wanted information from this record

When detail is supplied, this refines as below.

1.1 *Index* ← 0
2.1 **loop while** *TimeTable*[*Index*].*Time* ≤ "09.00"
2.2   *Index* ← *Index* + 1
2.3 **loopend**
3.1 **loop while** *TimeTable*[*Index*].*Destination* ≠ "Blackpool"
3.2   *Index* ← *Index* + 1
3.3 **loopend**
4.1 write out "Departure time ", *TimeTable*[*Index*].*Time*
4.2 write out "From platform ", *TimeTable*[*Index*].*Platform*

□

This design may look like an acceptable solution to the posed task, but it contains one serious flaw. Can you see what it is? The algorithm assumes that there will *be* an entry in the table concerning a train to Blackpool after 09.00. Suppose there is no such train. The design will fail because *Index* will continue to increment until it gets beyond the size of the array, and there will be an 'out of range' error. (If you were to attempt to adapt the design so that it searches for the first train to *any* destination after *any* given time — these two pieces of information being provided by the user — then you really would have to cater for the possibility of there being no such train.)

The problem highlighted here has been a source of anguish for programmers over the years. Writing search algorithms would be so much easier if searches were always successful; but they are not. The design must always cater for the exceptional circumstances, and must certainly take into account the possibility of there being no match.

In the present example, the search will be known to be unsuccessful if a match has not been found by the time *Index* has reached *LastTrainIndex*.

There are numerous ways of building in a check for this occurrence. One elegant way is to employ a boolean variable that has initial value false and remains false until an attempt is made to increment *Index* beyond *LastTrainIndex*, signifying that no match has been found and that the search should come to an end. A suitable identifier for this boolean variable is *AtEnd*. Then, in the above design, the step

$$Index \leftarrow Index + 1$$

which occurs twice, may be replaced by the following steps.

if *Index* < *LastTrainIndex* **then**

   $Index \leftarrow Index + 1$

else

   $AtEnd \leftarrow$ true

ifend

An alternative, but less elegant, way is to add the condition
Index < *LastTrainIndex*
to the existing conditions in steps 2.1 and 3.1.

The boolean variable *AtEnd* will now play a part in control of each of the loops. If this variable ever acquires the value true, searching can be halted in the knowledge that there is no matching record in the table. Making use of it, see if you can adapt the earlier design to solve the following generalised version of the example.

Exercise 4.2

Write a design whose purpose is as follows. A destination and a time are to be read in from the keyboard. *TimeTable* is searched for the first train to that destination after that time. The design is to write out the departure time and platform of the first train or, if there is no such train, report this fact.

[*Solution on page 50*]

To round off this work on searching, you are invited to try your hand at implementing some simple linear searches. An initialised table is provided for you, in a program template. The table, called *Table*, is an array of 26 records each of which has two fields:

o a field of type *AnsiString*, with identifier *Name*;
o a field of type integer, with identifer *Age*.

The table is sorted by alphabetical ordering of the *Name* field.

No name appears more than once.

Your task, in the computing activity which follows shortly, is to write some C++ code fragments to search the provided table. First, in Exercise 4.3, you should write a design for each fragment and plan the coding.

Exercise 4.3

Write a fragment of design to carry out each of the following tasks on the initialised table *Table* as described above.

(a) Display the contents of the table on the screen. That is, write out a list of all the names together with the associated ages.

(b) Search *Table* for a given age entered from the keyboard. All that is to be written out, apart from any prompt, are the names (if any) corresponding to that age.

(c) Search *Table* for a given name entered from the keyboard. The output is to consist of either the value in the *Age* field corresponding to this name or a message saying that the name does not appear in the table.

[*Solution on page 50*]

The following computing activity asks you to code, run and test your design fragment for part (c) of Exercise 4.3. You will need to plan the coding of the design fragment. The provided template initialises *Table*, so all that remains for you to do is add the other variable declarations and initialisations, and your code fragment. If you wish to repeat the activity to test parts (a) and (b) as well, by all means do so.

Computer Activity 4.1 _____

Open the project `Tablexxs.bpr`, which is to be found in the `Block II` folder. The file `TablexxsU.cpp` has already included the course team library MT262io and has some additional statements including

```
init(Table);
```

which initialises *Table*.

init is an example of a **function**. Functions will be discussed in some detail in the next unit.

The section where you are to write your code is clearly indicated. Enter your code for part (c) of Exercise 4.3, including the needed variable declarations, and run the program. After you have corrected any compilation errors, you can test the program by responding to the prompts. Amongst the test data, use the following names: "Black", "Cliff", "Aaron" and "Zynd". ("Aaron" is alphabetically before the first name in the table and "Zynd" is after the last, so these test extreme cases.)

[*Solution on page 53*]

4.3 A sorting algorithm

To complete this unit, one of many available algorithms for sorting a collection of data into some order will be discussed. This algorithm is known as **selection sort**. To illustrate this algorithm, suppose that you are given a collection of cards each of which has a whole number written on it, and that you have to sort the cards into increasing order. For example, consider the nine cards illustrated below.

| 19 | 26 | 31 | 13 | 38 | 17 | 29 | 21 | 24 |

How would you go about sorting these into order? One approach would be to scan the cards to find the one with the largest number (in this case 38), and move that card to the end — its correct position. To be more careful, and not leave gaps in the sequence of cards, the best way of moving the largest card to the end is to have it swap places with the card currently at the end (in this case 24). Doing this — swapping the largest, 38, with the last, 24 — gives the following order.

| 19 | 26 | 31 | 13 | 24 | 17 | 29 | 21 ‖ 38 |

unsorted part

The final card is now in its sorted position, but the front eight remain unsorted. Next apply the original step to the unsorted part. That is, find the card with the largest number in the unsorted part (in this case 31) and move it to its correct position by swapping it with the last one in the unsorted part, namely 21. The result is as follows.

| 19 | 26 | 21 | 13 | 24 | 17 | 29 ‖ 31 | 38 |

unsorted part

Continuing in this way, at the next stage 29 is the largest number remaining in the unsorted part and this card is in last position, so it swaps with itself.

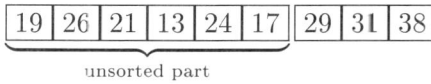

| 19 | 26 | 21 | 13 | 24 | 17 || 29 | 31 | 38 |

$\underbrace{\qquad\qquad\qquad\qquad}_{\text{unsorted part}}$

Exercise 4.4

Trace this selection sort through to completion. At each stage, look at the unsorted part and swap the card with the largest number with the one in last position, and then reduce the unsorted part by one card.

[*Solution on page 52*]

The next step is to write a general design for the algorithm used in the card-sorting example. Although the example used integer values, the algorithm can be applied to any kind of data on which there is a well-defined ordering. To highlight this point, the algorithm will be designed for an array of string, rather than integer, values. (This same algorithm could equally well be adapted to sort a table by imposing an ordering on the records in the table as implied by the ordering of one of its fields.)

Although the example is sorting a collection of cards with numbers on them, you may recognise it as a model of an array of integers. Swapping cards is essentially swapping the contents at appropriate indexes of an array.

Example 4.3 Sorting a string array

Write a design to sort a given array of string values into increasing order. □

To give some specific context assume that the array of strings is declared by

```
AnsiString MyArray[Size];
```

where *Size* is some (positive) integer constant.

The array index values will be from 0 to $Size - 1$.

The following top-level design summarises the essence of the algorithm illustrated above.

1   initialise variables
2   **loop for** each unsorted part in turn
3   find largest element in unsorted part
4   swap this largest element with last element of unsorted part
5   **loopend**

In the context of string values, the *largest* refers to the *last in order*.

There is the tricky matter to resolve of how to represent the unsorted part. Originally, the unsorted part consists of the whole array, that is, the part from index 0 to index $Size - 1$. Subsequently, on completion of each pass of the loop (in step 2), the unsorted part gets smaller in that the largest index value of the unsorted part is decremented by 1. Thus it is reasonable to introduce an integer variable *TopOfUnsorted*, say, so that the unsorted part will consist of the array elements at indexes from 0 to *TopOfUnsorted*. Initially, *TopOfUnsorted* will be set to $Size - 1$, and will come down in steps of 1. The final pass of the loop will involve an unsorted part consisting of indexes from 0 to 1 inclusive. Iteration will halt when *TopOfUnsorted* becomes 0. Thus the loop condition for step 2 is now decided.

2.1   **loop for** *TopOfUnsorted* ← *Size* − 1 **to** 1

The difficult step for refinement is going to be step 3. The purpose of step 3 is to find the largest (i.e. last alphabetically) element in the unsorted part of the array. A linear search of the part of the array from index 0 to index *TopOfUnsorted*, keeping track of the largest found so far, will do the trick. From the discussion above, it is the *position* (i.e. index) of the largest element in the unsorted part that is required, not the actual largest value. Knowing the position is enough to enable the swapping to be done.

This suggests that a further variable *IndexOfLargest*, say, to hold the index at which the largest element in the unsorted part resides, will be required.

Initially, *IndexOfLargest* will need to be set to 0.

The following figure illustrates the variables introduced above, in the context of an array of string values that are types of animal.

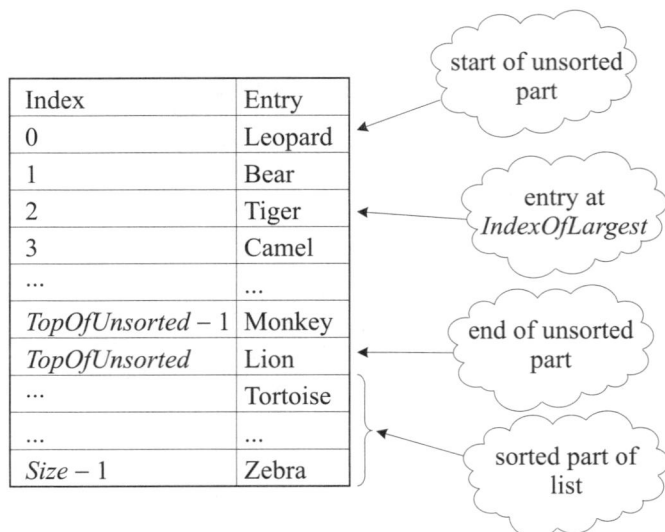

Index	Entry
0	Leopard
1	Bear
2	Tiger
3	Camel
...	...
TopOfUnsorted – 1	Monkey
TopOfUnsorted	Lion
...	Tortoise
...	...
Size – 1	Zebra

start of unsorted part

entry at *IndexOfLargest*

end of unsorted part

sorted part of list

The purpose of step 3 of the design is to find *IndexOfLargest*. The following refinement is a linear search to do exactly that.

3.1   *IndexOfLargest* ← 0
3.2   **loop for** *Index* ← 1 **to** *TopOfUnsorted*
3.3   **if** *MyArray*[*Index*] > *MyArray*[*IndexOfLargest*] **then**
3.4   *IndexOfLargest* ← *Index*
3.5   **ifend**
3.6   **loopend**

The loop checks each element of the unsorted part in turn: if that element is the largest so far, the index of that element is assigned to *IndexOfLargest*. When the loop finishes, the wanted index is *IndexOfLargest*.

Five variables have now appeared, so they should be recorded in a data table. Although the value of *Size* does not change throughout the program (it is constant), it makes the program more easily adaptable to (different sized arrays) to use a variable to store the value. The fact that the value is intended to remain fixed is noted in the data table.

Type	Identifier	Description
Integer (constant)	*Size*	The size of the array to be sorted
Array of string	*MyArray[Size]*	The array to be sorted
Integer	*TopOfUnsorted*	Indexes 0 to *TopOfUnsorted* are unsorted
Integer	*IndexOfLargest*	Index of the largest element of unsorted part
Integer	*Index*	Loop control variable used in search of unsorted part

Exercise 4.5 asks you to complete the design. The refinement of steps 2 and 3 have been discussed above. In refining step 4, do remember that care is needed in swapping two elements of an array.

You may wish to refer to Exercise 2.3 for swapping array elements.

Exercise 4.5 ⎯⎯⎯⎯⎯⎯⎯⎯⎯⎯⎯⎯⎯⎯⎯⎯⎯⎯⎯⎯⎯

Complete the design to solve the string array sorting problem. You do not need to worry about initialisation of *MyArray* and *Size*, as you may assume that is done separately.

[*Solution on page 52*]

To illustrate the selection sort algorithm, the course team has written a program to sort the table of Computer Activity 4.1. There, the table was sorted by the values in the *Name* field. The program, which is the subject of Computer Activity 4.2, reorganises the table so that the records are in increasing order of age. The code is derived from the design reached in Exercise 4.5, but with *MyArray* replaced by *Table* and *Size* by the specific value 26.

Computer Activity 4.2 ⎯⎯⎯⎯⎯⎯⎯⎯⎯⎯⎯⎯⎯⎯⎯⎯⎯

Open and run the project CTTabsrt.bpr Note how the 26 records are sorted by age.

Inspect the code file to convince yourself it is a coding of a design like the one in the solution to Exercise 4.5.

What is the purpose of the last **if** statement in the code?

[*Solution on page 53*]

Objectives

After studying this unit, you should be able to:

o create structure definition tables for records and write structure definitions in C++, declaring variables in course style;

o use assignment and equality of records appropriately in designs and code those designs;

o declare in C++: arrays of built-in or programmer defined base type, tables, and two-dimensional arrays;

o manipulate elements in an array;

o use the dot notation for fields of a record or table;

o use **for** loops in design, and code such designs;

o use all the above ideas in solving problems;

o follow the design and coding of a linear search;

o describe the operation of the selection sort algorithm on an array;

o use and understand the use of the following terms: record, record type definition, structure definition, record structure, record variable, type name, field, dot notation for fields, array, base type of an array, table, database, two-dimensional array, **for** loop, **for** statement, linear search, selection sort.

Solutions to the Exercises

Section 1

Solution 1.1
The *EmployeeType* will be a record type with five fields for which the course team has chosen identifiers *Name, Dept, Years, Status* and *Salary*. The type of *Status* has been taken to be character, the values being M (for married), S (for single) and D (for divorced). The *Salary* field could be either of type real, as below, or integer.

Structure definition	*EmployeeType*	
Type	Field identifier	Description
String	*Name*	Name of employee
String	*Dept*	Department of employee
Integer	*Years*	Number of completed years of service
Character	*Status*	Marital status: 'M', 'S' or 'D'
Real	*Salary*	Annual salary in pounds

Solution 1.2
The cursor position is determined by a pair of integer values, namely its row number and its column number. This suggests defining a type *CursorPosType*, say, as follows.

Structure definition	*CursorPosType*	
Type	Field identifier	Description
Integer	*Row*	Row number (1 to 25) for position on screen
Integer	*Column*	Column number (1 to 80) for position on screen

(It would be possible to hold the position as a single integer in the range 1 to 2000, supported by software to extract the row and column numbers. However, the record structure has many advantages, including the fact that it models the description of the screen more closely than the single integer suggestion.)

Solution 1.3

The structure will have to hold a field for each of the six numbers chosen, for the number of draws covered, for the type of draw covered, and for the submitted date.

Structure definition	*NLEntryType*	
Type	Field identifier	Description
Integer	*Choice1*	First choice (1 to 49) for draw
Integer	*Choice2*	Six distinct ...
Integer	*Choice3*	...
Integer	*Choice4*	...
Integer	*Choice5*	...
Integer	*Choice6*	... choices in all
Integer	*NumberOfDraws*	Number of draws (1 to 8) to be covered
Character	*WedOrSat*	'W' (for Wed), 'S' (for Sat) or 'B' (for Both)
String	*Date*	Date entry is submitted in 19/11/2012 format

Solution 1.4

1.1   *FJRec.Name* ← "Frank Jones"

1.2   *FJRec.Address* ← "26 Lomaria Avenue, Oldtown"

1.3   *FJRec.PostCode* ← "TN2 3ZN"

1.4   *FJRec.Gender* ← 'M'

1.5   *FJRrec.Age* ← 34

1.6   *FJRec.TeleNo* ← "01987 654321"

Note that it is good practice to assign values to fields in the order in which the fields appear in the structure definition.

Solution 1.5

(a) The row number is referred to as *ArrowPos.Row*, and the column number is referred to as *ArrowPos.Column*.

(b) To move one place up the screen, the row number is decreased by 1. If the row number is currently 1, such a move cannot be made. Similarly, to move one place to the right, the column number is increased by 1, and this will be possible except when the column number is already 80. Therefore the following design will achieve the desired result.

1.1   **if** *ArrowPos.Row* > 1 **then**

1.2   *ArrowPos.Row* ← *ArrowPos.Row* − 1

1.3   **ifend**

2.1   **if** *ArrowPos.Column* < 80 **then**

2.2   *ArrowPos.Column* ← *ArrowPos.Column* + 1

2.3   **ifend**

Alternative conditions for the **ifs** are *ArrowPos.Row* ≠ 1 and *ArrowPos.Column* ≠ 80.

(c) The position at the bottom left has row number 25 and column number 1. Therefore, a suitable design is as follows.

1   *ArrowPos.Row* ← 25

2   *ArrowPos.Column* ← 1

If these two instuctions are reversed in order, the overall effect is the same.

Solution 1.6

(a) Valid

(b) Invalid (*HisRecord* and *MyRecord* are of different types, so the assignment is invalid.)

(c) Invalid (The comparison < does not apply to records.)

(d) Valid

Solution 1.7

(a) The records (for each item) will have four fields.

```
struct  ItemType
{
 AnsiString  Code;
 int  StockLevel;
 int  UnitCost;
 AnsiString  Supplier;
};

ItemType SmallTable;
ItemType NewTable;
ItemType SoftSofa;
```

(The course style is to have separate declarations for each variable as above, but

```
ItemType SmallTable, NewTable, SoftSofa;
```

is also correct C++ code.)

(b)
```
SmallTable.Code = "TB56";
SmallTable.StockLevel = 50;
SmallTable.UnitCost = 299;
SmallTable.Supplier = "Tableland";
```

(c) There is no need to copy the field values one by one; record assignment is allowed since *SmallTable* and *NewTable* are of the same type.

```
NewTable = SmallTable;
```

(d)
```
SoftSofa.StockLevel = SoftSofa.StockLevel - 1;
```

(e)
```
if (SoftSofa.StockLevel < 5)
    WriteStringPr("Stock level is low on  ", SoftSofa.Code);
```

Section 2

Solution 2.1

(a) The required code is

```
int Count[100];
```

(b) *Count*[27] is the identifier (name) of the integer variable at index 27 of the array `Count`.

Solution 2.2

(a) The array *MyNumbers*, say, has to hold six values of type integer, so the following does what is required.

```
int MyNumbers[6];
```

(b) The base type could be either integer or real as you were not told whether temperatures are being read to the nearest whole degree or to one (or more) decimal places. (Presumably the specification for the problem in which this arose would settle the choice, and specify the temperature scale.) With temperatures recorded as reals, the array (which could be called *Readings*) has to contain 365 elements of this base type. So a suitable declaration is as follows.

```
float Readings[365];
```

(c) This can be stored as an array (called *League* below) of 18 records, where each record holds information on one team. To that end a structure definition is needed (called *TeamRecordType* below) to set up the base type for the array elements.

```
struct TeamRecordType
{
 AnsiString Name;
 int   Played;
 int   Won;
 int   Drawn;
 int   Lost;
 int   Points;
};

TeamRecordType League[18];
```

Solution 2.3

There is a temptation to swap the two elements by means of the pair of assignment steps

1    $Ladder[5] \leftarrow Ladder[6]$
2    $Ladder[6] \leftarrow Ladder[5]$

But a moment's thought should reveal the flaw in this design. When the first assignment is executed the string value in $Ladder[6]$ is copied to $Ladder[5]$, at which point the original value in $Ladder[5]$ is lost. The same value is now in these two elements of $Ladder$ and the second assignment does not change anything.

The simple way round this is to use a temporary string variable, $Temp$, to store the value which would be lost by the first assignment, and then copy this preserved value in the second assignment, like this.

1    $Temp \leftarrow Ladder[5]$
2    $Ladder[5] \leftarrow Ladder[6]$
3    $Ladder[6] \leftarrow Temp$

($Temp$ would also have to be added to the data table.)

Solution 2.4

(a) 1 $Index \leftarrow 0$
    2   **loop while** $Index < 10$
    3.1 $YourArray[Index] \leftarrow MyArray[Index]$
    3.2 $Index \leftarrow Index + 1$
    4   **loopend**

(b) 1.1 $Equals \leftarrow$ true
    1.2 $Index \leftarrow 0$
    2   **loop while** $Index < 10$
    3.1   **if** $MyArray[Index] \neq YourArray[Index]$ **then**
    3.2 $Equals \leftarrow$ false
    3.3   **ifend**
    3.4 $Index \leftarrow Index + 1$
    4   **loopend**

Note that the course team decision to initialise $Equals$ as true simplifies the form of the **if** step.

You may feel, correctly, that this design would be better if the loop stopped as soon as an unequal pair of corresponding element values is found; that is, if ever $Equals$ becomes false. This is achieved by changing the loop condition as follows.

2   **loop while** ($Index < 10$) **and** ($Equals$)

Solution 2.5

(a) The information on Portugal is stored at index 9 in the table, so the name of its currency is held in the field $Exchange[9].Currency$.

(b) $Exchange[2].Rate$

(c) Each array element is a record with three fields. The one holding information on Germany is at index 5, so $Exchange[5]$ is the identifier of this record.

Solution 2.6

(a) The required declaration is

```
int AGrades[350][4];
```

If the order of the indexes is switched in the declaration, putting the [4] before the [350], then corresponding switches of the two indexes will be needed in part (b).

(b) (i) Because indexes start at 0, the answer is as follows.

```
AGrades[56][2]
```

(ii) As there are only four numbers to be averaged, it is feasible just to add them in a single expression, and then divide by 4. (This is just like the 'mean' problem considered in Section 1 of *Unit 1*, Block I.)

```
int Total;   // sum of the four grades for student number 37
float Mean;  // the mean grade for student number 37
 Total = AGrades[36][0] + AGrades[36][1] + AGrades[36][2] + AGrades[36][3];
 Mean = float(Total)/4;
```

However, the following is a more generally applicable approach, making use of a loop.

```
int Total;   // sum of the four grades for student number 37
int Index;   // loop control variable ranging over indexes 0 to 3
float Mean;  // the mean grade for student number 37
 Total = 0;
 Index = 0;
 while (Index < 4)
 {
   Total = Total + AGrades[36][Index];
   Index = Index + 1;
 }
 Mean = float(Total)/4;
```

Section 3

Solution 3.1

The loop control tells us that *Index* is going to start at -6 and increase in steps of 3 until it exceeds 6. That is, there will be passes of the loop with *Index* equal to $-6, -3, 0, 3$ and 6. On each pass, the value of $Index * (Index + 1)$ is written out; so the output will be

```
30   6   0   12   42
```

Solution 3.2

The integer variable *Index* is used for loop control in each part.

(a) 1   **loop for** *Index* ← 0 **to** 24
   2   *MyReals*[*Index*] ← 0
   3   **loopend**

(b) 1   **loop for** *Index* ← 0 **to** 24
   2   write out "Enter value for index ", *Index*
   3   read in *MyReals*[*Index*]
   4   **loopend**

(This design does not accommodate the customary colon following a prompt. One way of achieving this is to add the step

    write out ":";

immediately after step 2.)

Solution 3.3

(a) *Index* is initially 0 and increments by 2 on each pass of the loop until its value exceeds 9. At each pass, the string entry at the position of *Ladder* given by *Index* is written out. Thus the five string values are written out as follows.

```
Ladder[0]
Ladder[2]
Ladder[4]
Ladder[6]
Ladder[8]
```

> The carriage return ensures that each entry is on a separate line.

(b) This time *Index* is initially 10 and on completion of each pass of the loop it decrements by 1 until its value is less than 7. On each pass, two integers are written out: the current value of *Index* and the square of this value (separated by a space character). Hence four pairs of values are written out like this.

```
10 100
 9 81
 8 64
 7 49
```

(c) The purpose of this fragment of code is to write out the first (in alphabetical order) name in *Ladder*.

This can be seen by tracing the code (informally). It begins with the declaration of an integer variable *First*, which is initially 0. Then comes the **for** loop. The control statement tells us that *Index* will run through successive values from 1 to 9 inclusive. The loop body consists of a single **if** statement; if the value of the element of *Ladder* at position given by *Index* is less than (that is, alphabetically before) the element of *Ladder* at position given by *First*, then *First* is updated to hold this value of *Index*. So each element in turn is inspected to see if it is the first (alphabetically) so far, and *First* keeps track of the index where the first in alphabetical order has been found. On completion of the loop, the value of this first element is written out.

> String order is essentially alphabetical here since the elements in *Ladder* are surnames of people.

Solution 3.4

(a)

```
int I;      // The control variable has to be declared.
 for (I = 1; I <= 20; I = I + 1)
 {
   WriteInt(I);
   WriteChar(' ');
   WriteFloatCr(float(1)/I);
 }
```

An alternative for the last two write out statements is the following single statement.

```
   WriteFloatPrCr(" ", float(1)/I);
```

(b)

```
int Index;
 for (Index = 9; Index > 0; Index = Index - 2)
   WriteStringCr(Ladder[Index]);
```

Solution 3.5

The array *Frequency* has base type integer, so its type is 'Array of integer'. The data table entry is as follows.

Type	Identifier	Description
Array of integer	*Frequency*[11]	Array holding counts of each grade

The C^{++} declaration is

```
int Frequency[11];
```

Solution 3.6

To answer this exercise, you might use a pre-conditioned or a post-conditioned loop, with further choices still to be made. However, do be careful to make sure that the sentinel input is not counted. If you read in the next grade at the start of the loop body, you will need an **if** in the loop body to bypass the counting steps when the sentinel is entered.

Make sure that your design does not include a reference to *Frequency*[999]!

The course team solution (below) avoids the need for an **if** by reading in the first grade prior to entering the loop and then placing the read-in step at the end of the loop body. In this way, loop control tests for entry of the sentinel immediately.

2.1   write out "Enter first grade: "

2.2   read in *Grade*

2.3   **loop while** *Grade* $\neq$ 999

3.1   *CountOfGrades* $\leftarrow$ *CountOfGrades* + 1

3.2   *Frequency*[*Grade*] $\leftarrow$ *Frequency*[*Grade*] + 1

3.3   write out "Enter next grade or 999 to terminate: "

3.4   read in *Grade*

4   **loopend**

Solution 3.7

A range check which ensures the number lies between 0 and 10 inclusive will remove the possibility of 999 being entered as the first grade (as well as detecting other user errors).

2.2.1 read in *Grade*

2.2.2 **loop while** (*Grade*< 0) **or** (*Grade* > 10)

2.2.3   write out "Invalid number. Please enter again: "

2.2.4   read in *Grade*

2.2.5 **loopend**

An alternative condition for step 2.2.2 is *Grade* = 999.

Section 4

Solution 4.1

In this case, a step 1 is needed to read in the required destination. The only other change involves replacing "Blackpool" in step 3.1. The following design

1.1   write out "Enter destination: "

1.2   read in *PlaceWanted*

2.1   **loop for** *Index* ← 0 **to** *LastTrainIndex*

3.1   **if** *TimeTable*[*Index*].*Destination* = *PlaceWanted* **then**

3.2   write out *TimeTable*[*Index*].*Time*

3.3   **ifend**

4   **loopend**

codes as

```
// TimeTable declared, as given in text, and initialised
AnsiString PlaceWanted;
int Index;
  PlaceWanted = ReadStringPr("Enter destination: ");
  for (Index = 0; Index <= LastTrainIndex; Index = Index + 1)
    if (TimeTable[Index].Destination == PlaceWanted)
        WriteStringCr(TimeTable[Index].Time);
```

Solution 4.2

The following design uses string variables *Place* and *AfterTime* for the two user inputs.

1.1	write out "Enter required destination: "
1.2	read in *Place*
1.3	write out "Enter earliest time wanted: "
1.4	read in *AfterTime*
2.1	*Index* ← 0
2.2	*AtEnd*← false
3.1	**loop while**
	not *AtEnd* **and** (*TimeTable*[*Index*].*Time* ≤ *AfterTime*)
3.2	**if** *Index* < *LastTrainIndex* **then**
3.3	*Index* ← *Index* + 1
3.4	**else**
3.5	*AtEnd* ← true
3.6	**ifend**
3.7	**loopend**
4.1	**loop while**
	not *AtEnd* **and** (*TimeTable*[*Index*].*Destination* ≠ *Place*)
4.2	**if** *Index* < *LastTrainIndex* **then**
4.3	*Index* ← *Index* + 1
4.4	**else**
4.5	*AtEnd* ← true
4.6	**ifend**
4.7	**loopend**
5.1	**if** *AtEnd* = true **then**
5.2	write out "There are no such trains."
5.3	**else**
5.4	write out "Departs ", *TimeTable*[*Index*].*Time*
5.5	write out " from platform ", *TimeTable*[*Index*].*Platform*
5.6	**ifend**

Solution 4.3

The following variables, in addition to *Table*, are used in the solution given below.

Type	Identifier	Description
String	*NameWanted*	Name input by user
Integer	*AgeWanted*	Age input by user
Boolean	*AtEnd*	Set to true if end of table is reached
Integer	*Index*	Loop control variable, 0 to 25

(a) This is a straightforward application of a **for** loop. Each of the 26 records is accessed in turn, and the two field values written out.

1	**loop for** *Index* ← 0 **to** 25
2	write out *Table*[*Index*].*Name*, *Table*[*Index*].*Age*
3	**loopend**

(b) Once again, the whole table has to be visited, so a **for** loop is employed; but this time the search is for a specific value in the *Age* field.

1.1   write out "Enter age required: '
1.2   read in *AgeWanted*
1.3   write out " Names with this age are: "
2.1   **loop for** *Index* ← 0 **to** 25
3.1   **if** *Table*[*Index*]*.Age* = *AgeWanted* **then**
3.2   write out *Table*[*Index*]*.Name*
3.3   **ifend**
3.4   **loopend**

It may happen that no names are written out!

(c) This time a conditioned loop is needed because the search can halt as soon as the match is found. (Recall that no name appears more than once.) But notice that, even if there is no match, it might not be necessary to search right to the end of the table. It will be known that the search is unsuccessful once you get beyond (alphabetically) the place in the table where the required name ought to be. For example, if you are searching for "Gray" and reach "Harris", then you know that "Gray" is not there, and so you need not check the remaining entries. Nevertheless, you must still make sure you do not drop off the end of the table; you might be asked to search for "Zynd"!

Here is the course team's design. Note how step 2.1 controls the search loop, and that step 5.1 is necessary to check the success, or otherwise, of the search.

1.1   write out "Enter wanted name: "
1.2   read in *NameWanted*
1.3   *Index* ← 0
1.4   *AtEnd* ← false
2.1   **loop while**
              not *AtEnd* **and** (*Table*[*Index*]*.Name* < *NameWanted*)
3.1   **if** *Index* < 25 **then**
3.2   *Index* ← *Index* + 1
3.3   **else**
3.4   *AtEnd* ← true
3.5   **ifend**
4   **loopend**
5.1   **if** *Table*[*Index*]*.Name* = *NameWanted* **then**
5.2   write out "Age is ", *Table*[*Index*]*.Age*
5.3   **else**
5.4   write out "Name is not in table."
5.5   **ifend**

Solution 4.4

At the next stage 26 swaps with 17.

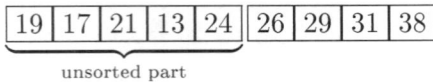

| 19 | 17 | 21 | 13 | 24 | 26 | 29 | 31 | 38 |

unsorted part

Then 24 swaps with itself.

| 19 | 17 | 21 | 13 | 24 | 26 | 29 | 31 | 38 |

unsorted part

Then 21 swaps with 13.

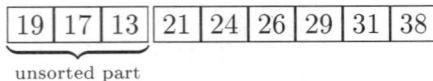

| 19 | 17 | 13 | 21 | 24 | 26 | 29 | 31 | 38 |

unsorted part

Then 19 swaps with 13.

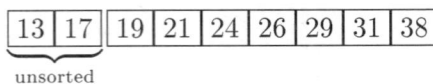

| 13 | 17 | 19 | 21 | 24 | 26 | 29 | 31 | 38 |

unsorted

In fact, the collection is now sorted, but as there remain two elements in the unsorted part there will be one final step: 17 swaps with itself. The process will, in general, stop when there is just one element remaining in the unsorted part.

Solution 4.5

In fact, as *MyArray* and *Size* are initialised separately, and *IndexOfLargest* is initialised in step 3.1, there are no initialisations required; so step 1 disappears at refinement. One further variable is needed in refining step 4 — a string variable, *TempStr*, to hold temporarily one of the values during a swap.

2.1 **loop for** $TopOfUnsorted \leftarrow Size - 1$ **to** 1
3.1 $IndexOfLargest \leftarrow 0$
3.2 **loop for** $Index \leftarrow 1$ **to** $TopOfUnsorted$
3.3 **if** $MyArray[Index] > MyArray[IndexOfLargest]$ **then**
3.4 $IndexOfLargest \leftarrow Index$
3.5 **ifend**
3.6 **loopend**
4.1 $TempStr \leftarrow MyArray[TopOfUnsorted]$
4.2 $MyArray[TopOfUnsorted] \leftarrow MyArray[IndexOfLargest]$
4.3 $MyArray[IndexOfLargest] \leftarrow TempStr$
5   **loopend**

Solutions to the Computer Activities

Section 3

Solution 3.1

If you get into difficulty, you can compare your program with that of the course team by opening the project CTGrades.bpr, which is in the Block II folder.

You may wish only to open the file CTGradesU.cpp (use File|Open...) to compare the course team's code with yours.

Section 4

Solution 4.1

If you have difficulty with the details, there is a complete working version in the project CTTabexs.bpr in the Block II folder. The file CTTabexsU.cpp is the one to open if you just wish to compare your code with the course team version. This program contains code for all three parts of Exercise 4.3.

Solution 4.2

The two **for** loops used in the design in the solution to Exercise 4.5 are present, the inner one including an **if** statement as there.

The program window accommodates only 25 lines of text. The purpose of the final **if** statement is to cater for this, and to draw the user's attention to the fact that the initial list is not complete.

The number of lines may vary according to how various *Windows* options have been set.

Index